"The Little Girls Story"

Urel's Jamaica House

By: Anya Mattis

Copyright© 2018 Anya Mattis

All Rights Reserved. No part of this publication may be reproduced, distributed, or transmitted in any form or by any means, including photocopying, recording, or other electronic or mechanical methods, without the prior written permission of the publisher, except in the case of brief quotations embodied in critical reviews and certain other noncommercial uses permitted by copyright law.

I dedicate this book to my mom and dad because they help me to reach for the stars. They often say, "when you use your mind it's nothing you can't do in life." I love them so much.

Once upon a time there was a little girl named Anya. I am Anya.

When I was five, I asked my dad if he could open a restaurant called, "Urel's Jamaican Kitchen".
He said, "one day stinky".
Stinky, is our little fun name.

When I was six, my dad really worked hard to open the restaurant for my little brother and me. His job was detailing cars.

My dad would let my little brother and I come and help him detail cars. It was so much fun, but very hot and tiring.

When I was seven, my dad told my older brother Elisha that he was going to work in the restaurant. I said, "WHAT RESTAURANT"? Daddy said, "That's the surprise!"

My dad's restaurant finally opened
on January 10, 2018.
I'm very proud of my dad and that my dream came true. I've learned how to work the register at my dad's restaurant and I enjoy helping all the customers.

Now the restaurant is a big success. You should come and check it out!

About the Author

Anya Mattis is 8 years old and the eighth of nine children. Anya started writing at the age of five years old and has a love of being creative. She has explored her creative side and have put her thoughts on paper to create several children's stories, which are to come. In her free time, she enjoys competition cheerleading, gymnastics, and all school sponsored activities such as talent shows and the spelling bee each year. She's also the big sister to her 5-year-old baby brother Carter.

www.ingramcontent.com/pod-product-compliance
Lightning Source LLC
Chambersburg PA
CBHW060202429042
44108CB00024B/2769